the true book of

Spinoffs from Space

By Leila Boyle Gemme

All photographs courtesy of
National Aeronautic and Space Administration

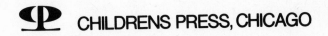 CHILDRENS PRESS, CHICAGO

Cover photo: Volunteers from the Houston Fire Department during a test of firefighter clothing made from non-flammable space-age fabrics.
Frontispiece: Astronaut Edwin E. Aldrin, Jr. on the moon. The Lunar Module, with the flag of the United States nearby, can be seen in the center background.

Library of Congress Cataloging in Publication Data

Gemme, Leila B.
  The true book of spinoffs from space.

  SUMMARY: Describes some of the inventions resulting from the space program that have proved useful on earth.
    1. Technology—transfer—Juvenile literature.
[1. Technology transfer] I. Title.
T174.3.G44   600   76-49936
ISBN 0-516-01209-6

CONTENTS

Astronaut Edwin E. Aldrin, Jr., Apollo 11 Lunar Module pilot,
on the surface of the moon. The lunar module is on the left.

WHAT IS A SPACE SPINOFF?

The space program was begun so men could be sent to the moon. The first two men landed there in 1969.

It was a great adventure. The men who went to the moon made new discoveries about it.

Other discoveries were made because of the space program. Very special ships had to be built to send men to the moon. New kinds of tools had to be invented.

Some of these new inventions could be used on earth. This book tells about the inventions that men could use on earth.

We call these inventions "spinoffs" of the space program.

Opposite: The Apollo 11 space vehicle lifts off the launching pad to begin man's first lunar landing mission.

This fireman is using a lightweight air tank (breathing system) as he works to put out a fire. His job is easier because the new air tank is small and weighs thirteen pounds less than other air tanks.

SPINOFFS FOR SAFETY

Men in space need to carry air tanks. The air tanks must be very small. But there were no small air tanks. The scientists of the space program built new ones. They weighed thirteen pounds less than other air tanks. They also held more air.

This invention could be used on earth, too. The new small air tanks helped to make the work of firemen easier.

Firemen often must enter a burning building. An air tank can be a big help when a fireman does this. But the old, bulky air tanks made the work harder. Many firemen did not want to use them.

Then firemen learned about the new air tanks. They were lighter. They held more air. Firemen liked to use them. Soon the air tanks used by the men in space were found in firehouses. They were spinoffs of the space program.

These three NASA (National Aeronautics and Space Agency) firemen are using lightweight breathing systems as they work to put out a fire.

The clothes these firemen are wearing are made from space-age
fabrics that will not burn. They make it possible for the
firemen to come very close to the fire without being burned.

Later new face masks, harnesses, and clothes were made for firemen. The ideas for these came from space suits, too.

The firemen in this picture are wearing clothes made of space-age fabrics that will not burn. They are made of many layers of fabrics and insulation. They are like the clothes that men in spacecraft must wear. In a spacecraft there is great danger from fire because the oxygen level inside the spacecraft is very high. Oxygen burns very easily. That is why these fire-resistant fabrics were invented.

At NASA (the National Aeronautics and Space Agency), men found other inventions that could be used for different kinds of emergencies. Doctors needed to know about the health of the men during a space flight. They wanted to know their heart rates. Their blood pressure was important. They also needed to know if they were breathing properly.

The researchers developed tools that could send medical information across thousands of miles.

Today those tools are used on city streets. Rescue workers carry a **portable ambulance module.** Wires from this metal box can be attached to a sick person's body.

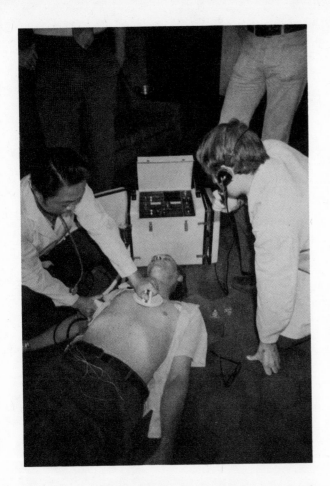

Medical technicians are stimulating the patient's heart. The man at the right is in radio contact with a doctor who will be able to tell the technicians what to do to help the patient.

Medical information from the sick person is sent to the doctor in the hospital. The doctor tells the rescue workers what to do. Many lives have been saved using these tools.

This life raft was developed by NASA for use by the astronauts. It was later made to be used by the Coast Guard, navies, merchant marines, and pleasure boatmen. It is lightweight, can be inflated, does not tip over, and can be seen on radar.

We are safer on the ocean because of space spinoffs.

When men return from space, they splash down in the ocean. To help find them quickly, NASA built a special life raft. It was made from a new material. This material can be seen from far away. It is seen on a special screen called radar.

Now this material is used in life rafts that people store in their boats. Rescues at sea are more likely to happen because of this special material.

There is less danger of certain kinds of fire now, too. NASA made a new kind of foam coating. It was invented to lower the fire danger in spacecraft. Today it is sprayed onto small boats. Now they do not burn so easily.

This small boat is being sprayed with "Flamarest," a coating that will keep the boat from burning if a fire starts in it.

A fire-index monitor keeps a check on air temperature, relative humidity, and dryness of the litter on the ground in a forest. The information is beamed to a satellite, then to a NASA station, and then to a forest-ranger station. In this way, forest rangers always know where there is a fire or danger of a fire starting.

SPINOFFS THAT
HELP THE ENVIRONMENT

Some space spinoffs are being used to protect the things around us.

Fire is a danger to our forests. From NASA we have something new to help fight forest fires.

Scientists built tools to test the air and heat inside a spacecraft cabin. Later these tools were made into a machine. It is called a **fire index monitor.** In the forest it tests the air and the heat. It tells firemen where to keep close watch for fire.

Another machine used in spacecraft tells if there are harmful gases in the air. It is called a **spectrometer**. Now it is being changed so it will be able to detect any pollution in the air we breathe.

This spectrometer will be able to let us know
if there is pollution in the air that is being tested.

NASA'S Synchronous Meteorological Satellite (SMS-1) is about to be tested on a vibration table. It was launched May 17, 1974, and now sends back information about the weather all around the world.

Many kinds of satellites were sent into space. Some carried men to the moon. Others carried machines into space. These machines view the earth. They send back information about it.

One kind of satellite was built to watch the weather. It is called a **meteorological satellite.** It sends back facts about the weather all around the world.

LANDSAT I is a different kind of satellite. It sent back this picture. From the photograph scientists can tell where underground oil is located.

LANDSAT I sees many things. It helps to find air and water polluters. It can spot diseased trees in a forest.

Many problems on earth are more clear to man because of the space program.

LANDSAT I took this picture and sent it back to earth.
The "hazy" areas show where underground oil will probably be found.

Astronauts returning from the moon put on this Biological Isolation Garment (BIG) after splashdown. They wear it until they are in a special quarantine unit on a recovery ship. BIG keeps the wearer isolated from any germs in the air. It also keeps any germs the astronauts may have brought back from getting into the earth's air.

SPINOFFS FOR HEALTH

Doctors have been able to use many of the inventions from the space program.

Some people were afraid when men landed on the moon. They thought harmful germs might come from there.

So NASA scientists built a special suit. No germs could get in or out of this suit. The astronauts put it on after they splash down and wear it until they are in a special quarantine unit on the recovery ship.

That suit is called an isolation garment. Hospital patients will soon be able to use it. Some people get infections very easily. At this time, these people have to stay in one room by themselves. This room is protected from germs. Soon they will have isolation garments. They will be able to leave their special, protected rooms.

A coverall-type isolation suit like the one the little girl is
wearing will soon be available to patients who must be protected
from germs. A separate hood with a see-through face mask is attached
to the suit. Air is supplied through a tube attached to the hood.

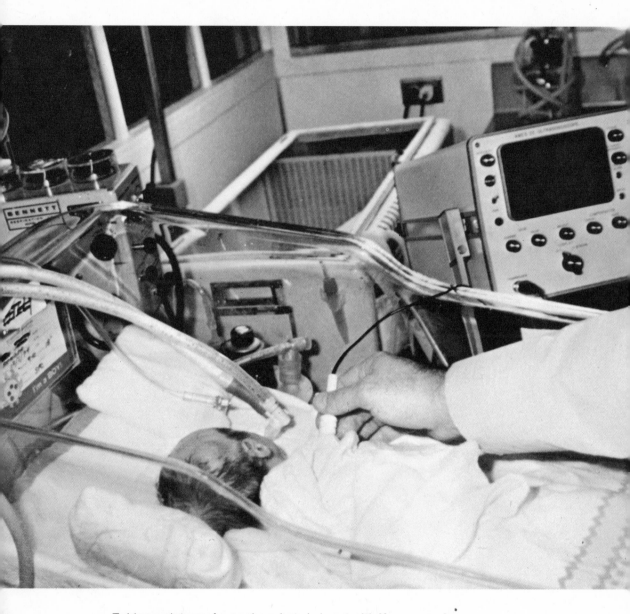

Taking a picture of a newborn baby's heart with X-rays can harm the baby. The device being used here takes a picture of the baby's heart with sonar. Very fast sound waves from the heart are sent back and form an image so doctors can keep a check on the heart.

Heart doctors use another space tool. Space scientists needed to know how the heart of an astronaut acted. X-rays were not possible in a spacecraft. So they planned a way to take a picture of the heart. They used sound waves. These pictures are called sonar images.

Doctors found that this new way to see the heart was useful. It is very good for the care of sick babies. In this picture, the baby's heart is being seen with sonar.

Another helpful spinoff is the heart pacemaker. The pacemaker is a tiny machine. It is put inside the body. There it helps to fix a heartbeat that is not steady. It must be very tiny.

Before the space program, it was not possible to build this kind of very small machine. But NASA learned how to build very small machines. This made it possible for a pacemaker to be built. Thousands of people depend on these tiny machines for their good health.

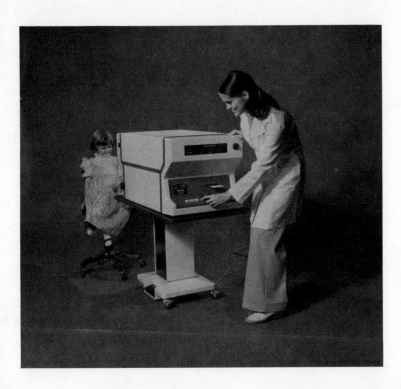

This automatic device works like a computer. An eye doctor who uses this can tell how to correct an eye problem in about three minutes. A regular eye test usually takes about ten or fifteen minutes.

Some space machines help doctors work more quickly and carefully.

The machine in this picture can check a person's eyes. It takes only a few seconds. It can "see" vision problems. It can also tell what kind of lens will fix them.

The foam used to make this wheelchair seat is three inches thick.
It is so comfortable that this girl can sit in her wheelchair for
as long as ten hours at a time without any soreness. The foam
is also being used for airplane seats and football helmet liners.

The space program built some things for comfort. One of these uses a new kind of plastic foam. NASA used it to make a better airplane seat.

Now it makes better wheelchair seats. The chair in the picture is made with the new foam. The girl can stay in her special foam seat three times longer than she could in her old one.

SPINOFFS FOR DAILY USE

Some things in our homes are changing because of the space program.

Foods are safer now. Many frozen foods have a special tag. It shows that they have stayed frozen.

The tag is made of crystals. The men at NASA were working on these crystals. They found that the crystals would change color if they were thawed. Later this discovery was made into a tag. This tag can protect us against unsafe frozen foods.

Foods have changed, too. We drink freeze-dried coffee. We make orange juice from a powder. Many of these new food processes were begun at NASA.

Left: This Radar Jac is warm when worn with one side out and cool when worn with the other side out. Its gold color can be seen clearly even when it is not daylight. The jacket also reflects radar rays.

Below: Many kinds of camping equipment and outdoor supplies for sportsmen are now made with insulated material developed by NASA. It is used to make blankets, ski parkas, and sleeping bags, as well as jackets.

Some of the clothes we play in have changed, too.

Skiers need to keep warm. Now there are boots and gloves that are run by batteries. They help to keep hands and feet much warmer in cold weather.

There are reversible jackets and blankets. With one side next to the body a sportsman can stay very warm. If the same side is outside, it reflects the sun's rays and keeps a sportsman very cool.

Some of the jackets can also be seen on radar. This could help find a person who is lost and needs to be rescued.

The idea for all these things came from space suits.

This picture shows a man hang gliding. Hang gliding is a new sport. The idea for the hang glider came from a special pair of wings. These wings were first built to use in recovering spacecraft.

Now hang gliders are used just for fun.

Hang gliding has become a popular sport. A special wing developed by NASA to use in recovering spacecraft is now used for fun.

About the Author

Leila Boyle Gemme was a high school teacher for several years before turning to writing. "When my children were born, I needed an 'at-home' career, and writing seemed like a good idea," she explains. She now presides over a lively household in Los Angeles, California, which includes a husband, three children, one dog, and currently, two goldfish. The subjects of her works are varied. Among other things, she has written about the sports world, entertainers, and, with this book, the space program.